Jonas Hartzel

A Dissertation on the First and Third Abrahamic Covenants

Jonas Hartzel

A Dissertation on the First and Third Abrahamic Covenants

ISBN/EAN: 9783337811556

Printed in Europe, USA, Canada, Australia, Japan

Cover: Foto ©Suzi / pixelio.de

More available books at **www.hansebooks.com**

A DISSERTATION

ON THE

FIRST AND THIRD ABRAHAMIC COVENANTS,

THE COVENANT OF HOREB

AND

THE NEW COVENANT.

THEIR DIFFERENTIAL PECULIARITIES.

BY

ELDER JONAS HARTZEL,

DAVENPORT, IOWA.

"Having no hope, and without God in the world."—PAUL.

SOLD BY

JAMES CHALLEN & SON, PHILADELPHIA,

SHELDON & CO., NEW YORK.—H. S. BOSWORTH, CINCINNATI,
AND THE AUTHOR, DAVENPORT, IOWA.

PUBLISHED BY T. HOLMAN,

CORNER OF CENTRE AND WHITE STREETS, NEW YORK.

1865.

PREFACE.

—

THE substance of the following pages was delivered in an extemporaneous discourse on the last Lord's day of August, 1864, before the Christian State Missionary Meeting, held at Columbus City, Iowa, by Elder Jonas Hartzel, and a copy was, by resolution of the meeting, unanimously required for publication, and the manuscript to be put into the hands of the Executive Board, and published under the auspices of the Society. But feeling that the object of the movers would be better accomplished by placing the whole matter into the hands of the author, he being willing to assume all responsibilities in the case, the Executive Board have cheerfully concurred in the arrangement. They would have published it as directed by the Society, believing it to be a valuable contribution to Christian literature, on a most important subject; but with the advice and concurrence of the author, they believe that the objects of the Society will be more fully accomplished by putting the matter under his direction and control. We commend it to the reading public and to the blessing of God.

JAMES CHALLEN, }
CHAS. LESSLIE, } *Executive Board.*
WM. GRAY, }

DAVENPORT, *June 6, 1865.*

THE COVENANTS.

"WHEREFORE remember, that ye being in time past Gentiles in the flesh, who are called uncircumcision by that which is called the circumcision in the flesh made by hands; that at that time ye were without Christ, being aliens from the commonwealth of Israel, and strangers from the covenants of promise, having no hope, and without God in the world. But now, in Christ Jesus, ye who sometimes were afar off are now made nigh by the blood of Christ." (Eph. ii., 11–13.)

"Having no hope, and without God in the world." This language is descriptive of the most forlorn condition ever contemplated. This state may be expressed, but not explained. If our imagination were improved a hundred-fold, and quickened to its highest point of capability, it would not be perception, it would be imagination still. Think of it—a people "having no hope, and without God in the world."

Of whom was this affirmed? Of ourselves. Of us, poor, helpless Gentiles. But why were our Gentile fathers "without hope and without God in the world?" Because they had no promise. But why had they no promise? Because they had no covenant—no covenant with God. The order is covenant, promise, hope, God!

No covenant, no promise, no hope, no God. The Jews had covenants ; they had promises, they had hope, they had God. They had God, as no people out of covenant could have God. They had God for all that the covenant was worth to them.

It is so commercially, as respects man with man.

There are commercial covenants, commercial promises, commercial hopes. You covenant with a man for money, or chattels ; out of that covenant arises a promise ; out of that promise originates a hope ; and you have the man pledged for all the covenant is worth. It may be one dollar, or it may be one thousand dollars.

But what is a covenant? A mutual contract or agreement of two or more persons to do or forbear some act or thing ; a contract, stipulation. The etymological meaning of the word is, a coming together. God and man have never come together in this world without covenants, however it may be in the world to come.

Hence the Gentiles having no covenant, they were "strangers," "aliens," "having no hope, and without God in the world." This was the condition of the Gentiles, of all the Gentiles. Before they could have hope or God in the world, they had to be brought into covenant, covenant relations, as we shall see.

In order that we may have a more full and satisfactory understanding of the subject, we must examine the records. Covenants usually are matters of record. There are many covenants in the Bible ; but there are only four that have a logical connection with the subject in hand. These are the first and the third covenants God made with Abraham, and what are in Bible language styled the "old" and "new" covenants. These we will examine in their order.

We now invite attention to the first : "Now the Lord had said unto Abram, Get thee out of thy country, and from thy kindred, and from thy father's house, unto a land that I will show thee : and I will make of thee a great nation, and I will bless thee, and make thy name great ; and thou shalt be a blessing : and I will bless them that bless thee, and curse him that curseth thee : and in thee shall all families of the earth be blessed." (Gen. xii., 1, 2, 3.) This promise is a covenant, and is so called in the New Testament.

Now it was for Abram to accept or reject the conditions of this covenant. If he had continued in his country, and in his father's house, there would have been no covenant, and Abram would have remained a hopeless and godless idolater. (See Joshua xxiv., 2.) "So Abram departed as the Lord had spoken unto him." Now Abram had a covenant ; he had promises, he had hope, he had God for the fulfillment of all these promises, and God had *the man* Abram, to use him for all the wise and beneficent purposes proposed to himself and mankind, both Jew and Gentile.

In this covenant we have all the germs of the remedial system. The salvation of the world was suspended on a fearful contingency, "to speak after the manner of men." How strong the attachments to country, to kindred, and to home ! What a conflict of motives were involved ! But with God there is no failure. The heart of Abram was in the hand of the Lord. God saw the end from the beginning. And that which was first in design was last in the execution : " In thee shall all families of the earth be blessed." "Praise the Lord all ye Gentiles, and laud him all ye people." This covenant was made with an individual. Note this fact. It will be of great importance in the elucidation of the subject.

Then God made another covenant with Abram : "And when Abram was ninety years old and nine, the Lord appeared to Abram, and said unto him, I am the Almighty God ; walk before me, and be thou perfect. And I will make my covenant between me and thee, and will multiply thee exceedingly. And Abram fell on his face : and God talked with him, saying, As for me, behold, my covenant is with thee, and thou shalt be a father of many nations. Neither shall thy name any more be called Abram, but thy name shall be Abraham ; for a father of many nations have I made thee. And I will make thee exceedingly fruitful, and I will make nations of thee, and kings shall come out of thee. And I will establish my covenant between me and thee and thy seed after thee in their generations, for an everlasting covenant, to be a God unto thee, and to thy seed after thee. And I will give unto thee, and to thy seed after thee, the land wherein thou art a stranger, all the land of Canaan, for an everlasting possession; and I will be their God. And God said unto Abraham, Thou shalt keep my covenant therefore, thou, and thy seed after thee in their generations. This is my covenant, which ye shall keep, between me and you and thy seed after thee: every man-child among you shall be circumcised. And ye shall circumcise the flesh of your foreskin; and it shall be a token of the covenant betwixt me and you. And he that is eight days old shall be circumcised among you, every man-child in your generations, he that is born in thy house, or bought with money of any stranger, which is not of thy seed. He that is born in thy house, and he that is bought with thy money, must needs be circumcised: and my covenant shall be in your flesh for an everlasting covenant. And the uncircumcised man-child, whose flesh of his foreskin is not circumcised, that soul shall be cut off from his people; he hath broken my covenant." (See Gen. xvii.)

In this covenant are a series of new promises: "Thou shalt be a father of many nations." "Kings shall come out of thee." "Be a God unto thee, and thy seed after thee." "I will give unto thee, and to thy seed, all the land of Canaan." We will not raise the question whether these promises are temporal or spiritual. They speak for themselves. There is no disagreement, save in this one: "I will be a God unto thee." Some assume that this is a promise of spiritual, of gospel blessings. But gospel blessings were promised in the first covenant; why repeat them in this? Paul says, "God preached the gospel to Abraham, *saying*, In thee shall all nations be blessed." (Gal. iii., 8.) But neither Paul nor any apostle ever once referred to this promise, "I will be a God unto thee, and thy seed after thee," as *having any relation to the gospel.* The natural and obvious meaning of the promise is this, "I will be a God unto thee, and thy seed after thee," in the fulfillment of all these promises. What I have promised to you, I, as your God, will, and I only can, accomplish for your children. Your children shall become "nations;" they shall beget "kings;" and they shall "possess all the land of Canaan." These conclusions were in the premises. Whether Abraham's logic, or any of his sons after him, understood any thing more, we leave to those who are interested in maintaining another interpretation to answer.

There are a few things in this covenant that claim special attention: 1. The charge, "Thou shalt keep my covenant." 2. "This is my covenant which ye shall keep."

The first charge is in the singular, the second is in the plural. "Ye," all the male members of his household. But what were they commanded to keep? Not the prom*ises. These were for God's keeping. What then? The condition of the covenant, whatever that might be, whether faith or piety, or something else.

"And ye shall circumcise the flesh of your foreskin" is the only imperative in the covenant. This was the *only* condition of the covenant. This was the only act of obedience God required of Abraham; and a rigid test of *his faith it was.* But in this respect circumcision was to Abraham what it was to none of his household. Did Abraham accede to the proposed covenant? He did. The formal acceptance of the covenant is recorded in the words following: "In the selfsame day was Abraham circumcised, and Ishmael his son, and all the men of his house." This was the formal consummation. Now, God and Abraham had mutually recommitted themselves to each other. Abraham had God in additional promises and new hopes, and God had Abraham and his entire family; one family he claimed as his own. "*Let my people go.*" Oh, this covenanting

1*

with God! How vague are our conceptions, and how low our appreciation!

2. But where did God put this covenant—in the heart or in the flesh? In the flesh. "My covenant shall be in your flesh." But the covenant could be in the personal flesh of Abraham only during the period of his natural life, and as the covenant was to be an everlasting covenant it had to be placed in the flesh of his offspring. Hence the reason for the verse following in the connection. "And the uncircumcised man-child whose flesh of his foreskin is not circumcised, that soul shall be cut off from his people—he hath broken my covenant." The covenant in that case would not be in his "flesh," and consequently not in covenant with God. As this covenant was not in the heart, but in the flesh, it could as truly be in the flesh of Isaac when he was eight days old, as in the flesh of his father when he was ninety and nine years old. From a perversion of this have originated the notions of god-fathers—sanctified flesh, national religions, and state establishments, of which we shall hereafter speak.

3. This covenant took the whole family of Abraham in the aggregate. Its condition permitted this to be done, for the infant was as fitting a subject for circumcision as the mature man.

Out of this family grew a great and mighty nation, in covenant with God. And in the process of time his purposes required another covenant—a national covenant. To follow the order of history we shall refer to it.

"And Moses called all Israel, and said unto them: Hear, O Israel, the statutes and judgments which I speak in your ears this day, that ye may learn them, and keep and do them. The Lord our God made a covenant with us in Horeb. The Lord made not this covenant with our fathers, but with us, even us, who are all of us here alive this day." (Deut. v., 1, 2, 3.)

The definiteness of this statement is worthy of remark,

"not with our fathers, but with us, *even* us, *all* of us, who are *here alive* this day." The meaning of this language is, that God would take into covenant the whole nation in the concrete. It was a covenant with the circumcised seed of Abraham which had the token of a former covenant in their flesh,—"all of us, who are alive here this day." All, without respect to faith in God, moral condition, or character. This gave the covenant its national aspect. A single moral prerequisite, as faith in any proposition, or repentance for any sin, or obedience to any one commandment, would have made the covenant inapplicable to the nation in the aggregate. Indeed, the initiatives of any mere national religion must be based upon flesh. All the individuals of one nation may be the same in flesh, but never all the same in moral qualities. The inexorable necessity of this is seen in the fleshly basis of every State religion of the present time. You will ask, was there no personal obedience required by this covenant when accepted by the nation? Yes; the obligation to obey God had been created by a previous covenant in the flesh : "For I testify again to every man that is circumcised, that he is a debtor to do the whole law."

But God would not arbitrarily force this covenant upon the nation. He said unto them in the language of consultation, of great promise, and good hope : "Now, therefore, if ye will obey my voice indeed, and keep my covenant, then ye shall be a peculiar treasure unto me above all people : for all the earth is mine : And ye shall be unto me a kingdom of priests, and a holy nation. And all the people answered together, and said: All that the Lord hath spoken we will do. And Moses returned the words of the people unto the Lord." (Ex. xix., 5, 6, 8.) This was the formal acceptance of the covenant.

Now the nation had what no people under heaven had. They had a divine covenant, promises, hopes, and God ; and God had the nation for his "peculiar people." But no sooner had the nation pledged obedience than God uttered words of distrust. Hear him : "Oh, that there were such a heart in them, that they would fear me, and keep all my commandments always, that it might be well with them and with their children forever !" (Deut. v., 29.)

It was not long until every condition of this covenant was violated. One gathered "sticks on the Sabbath day;" another "blasphemed the name of the Lord ;" another "stole a wedge of gold ;" they made "graven images," etc. ; and the Lord said : "All the day long have I stretched out my hand to a disobedient and a gainsaying people."

The conditions of this covenant being violated, its promised blessings were forfeited ; and God determined that he would abrogate this national covenant and make a new one, not with the nation, but with individuals chosen out of the nation.

"Behold, the days come, saith the Lord, that I will make a new covenant with the house of Israel, and with the house of Judah : not according to the covenant that I made with their fathers, in the day that I took them by the hand to bring them out of the land of Egypt ; which my covenant they brake, although I was a husband unto them ('should I continue to be a husband unto them?' marginal reading), saith the Lord : But this shall be the covenant that I will make with the house of Israel : After those days, saith the Lord, I will put my law in their inward parts, and write it in their hearts ; and I will be their God, and they shall be my people. And they shall teach no more every man his neighbor, and every man his brother, saying, Know the Lord ; for they shall all know me, from the least of them unto the greatest of them, saith the Lord ; for I will forgive their iniquity, and I will remember their sin no more." (Jer. xxxi., 31–34.)

The importance of this new covenant in the present discussion demands a brief analysis.

What, then, is new in this covenant?

1. The place where this covenant should be "put" was new. One covenant, as we have seen, was put in the "flesh;" another, on tables of stone ; but of this the covenanter says : "I will put my law in their inward parts, and write it in their hearts."

By "inward parts" we may understand perception, conscience ; and by "hearts," the affections—perhaps all the intellectual and moral faculties of the soul—that part of humanity which is impressible, susceptible of divine influence. What follows justifies this view.

2. "And they shall teach no more every man his neighbor, and every man his brother, saying, Know the Lord, for they shall all know me," etc. There would be no occasion for this teaching, inasmuch as the covenant would be in the understanding and affections before they could be covenantees.

3. "I will forgive their iniquity, and remember their sins no more." This gracious promise is no part of any previous covenant, but the opposite—threatenings, terrible menaces. "I, the Lord thy God, am a jealous God, visiting the iniquities of the fathers upon the children," etc. Again : "The Lord will not hold him guiltless that taketh his name in vain." Punishment followed on the heels of transgression. But in the new, forgiveness takes the place of threatenings in the old. "I will write it in their hearts." Nothing engages the affections like forgiveness of sins.

See the two verses preceding the new covenant : "In those days they shall say no more : The fathers have eaten a sour grape, and the children's teeth are set on edge. But every one shall die for his own iniquity ; every man that eateth the sour grape, his teeth shall be set on edge." This popular Jewish adage shall not be used in the days of the new covenant.

"The fathers have eaten a sour grape, and the children's

teeth are set on edge" was, that the children " are bearing
the iniquity of their fathers." There seems to be something
exceedingly harsh in this feature of the old covenant. It
has been the subject of much cavil and infidel criticism.
But it was a most reasonable penalty. The children were
parties in the covenant through their fathers. They could
enjoy the promised blessings of the covenant in common
with their fathers ; the promises relating only to the good
things of this life, the children could enjoy the corn, the
wine, and the oil—they could " eat the fat and drink the
sweet." If they shared the good fortunes of their fathers,
why not their chastisements ? Besides, to set the children's
teeth on edge, because their fathers had foolishly eaten a
"sour grape," would serve as a healthful discipline, and
make them better men than their fathers were.

As the old covenant was based upon flesh, and as it took
the nation in the aggregate, the nation was blessed or
cursed, and each had to bear the iniquity of others, for the
good of the whole.

"Not according to the covenant I made with them when
I took them by the hand," etc. Therefore the specialties
of the "new" were to be unlike those of the "old." The
new covenant rests upon a new predicate ; upon personal
experience, " write it in their hearts ;" personal knowledge,
" for they shall all know me ;" and its provisions have
respect to personal guilt, " for I will forgive their iniquity ;" personal pardon, " I will remember their sin no more."

The new covenant could only take the house of Israel,
and the house of Judah in their individual capacity, and
as there is no proxy obedience in this it took every man
upon his own responsibility ; and as its promises are
spiritual it did not allow one man to bear the iniquity of
another, as this would have involved, guiltless, eternal
suffering ; and as this suffering would have to be inflicted
in a future life, it would be neither retributive nor dis-
ciplinary, but vindictive.

Has this prophecy been fulfilled? "Behold, the days come that I will make a new covenant," etc. We have been looking at prophecy, from prophecy we will pass to history.

In the days of Malachi, 397 years before Christ, the old national covenant was still in force. "Remember ye the law of Moses, my servant, which I commanded unto him in Horeb, for all Israel." (Mal. iv., 4.) This is the last prophetic admonition in the Old Testament.

John the Baptist was the next prophet sent to the nation. He never so much as alluded to the covenant of Sinai. Then followed Jesus. His mission was to the lost sheep of the house of Israel. He reproved the nation for its sins and apostasy from God. But he made no effort to call them back to the covenant God made with them in Horeb. In all his discourses he never once used the word covenant. This was a significant silence. Every prophet from Moses called attention to this covenant. But John and Jesus treated this covenant with respectful silence. This suggests that the old covenant was not to be enforced, and the time for the new had not yet come. Only once, before his ascension to heaven, did Jesus say covenant, and that was in this remarkable connection : "And he took the cup, and gave thanks, and gave it to them, saying, Drink ye all of it : for this is my blood of the new covenant, which is shed for many for the remission of sins." (Mat. xxvi., 27–28.) This is history, not prophecy. Jeremiah said, the "days will come ;" Jesus said, the days have come : "This is my blood of the new testament (covenant)." This reading is in the present tense, therefore, the beginning of the days of the new covenant. But there is no covenant here—no conditions, no promises, no acceptance. But there is a beautiful coincidence underlying the subject. It is the coincidence of type and antitype. Jesus and his disciples were now "eating the Passover." And as they were eating, "Jesus took bread," and immediately followed with the cup. The blood of the paschal lamb (of which the Passover supper was but a memorial), sprinkled upon the lintels and door-posts of the Israelites, saved them from the hand of avenging justice ; so the blood of Jesus Christ, "our passover," saves us from our sins. Remission of sins is a negation of justice. "For even Christ, our passover, is sacrificed for us." (1 Cor. v., 7.)

The passover lamb—its blood—the salvation by this— were types, of which Jesus is the perfect antitype. In allusion to this, Jesus is called the Lamb. "The Lamb slain for us." "The Lamb of God, that taketh away the sin of the world." The blood of the paschal lamb, and the salvation enjoyed by means of it, bore the same relation to the old covenant that the blood of Christ, and the salvation enjoyed by means of it, bear to the new covenant. Salvation from premature death of the first-born of Israel corresponds with their covenant, having promise of a long and happy life, as the blood of Christ and salvation from sin correspond with our covenant.

This coincidence also required a chronological agreement. Therefore, Jesus said on the same night, and the last time the paschal lamb was memorialized forever, "this cup is the new covenant in my blood ;" when, as yet, his blood was not shed in fact. If the cup could memorialize his blood after it was shed, it could before it was shed anticipate it. "This is my blood," was just as true, in a memorial sense, on the night before he died, as it is now. That he should have represented his blood then as shed, not before that night, nor afterward, is a fact of great chronological value. The blood of the paschal lamb was shed the night before the exodus of Israel. And in fifty days after their departure the old covenant was promulgated and accepted by the nation.

We here assume that, as the institution of the supper abolished forever the feast of unleavened bread, so the promulgation of the new covenant abolished forever the feast of Pentecost.

"For this is my blood of the new covenant, which is shed for many for the remission of sins." The wording of the new covenant, as we have seen, excludes the idea of national aggregation. Moses said to the nation, the "Lord made this covenant with us, *even* us, who are all of *us here alive this day.*" Language can not more strongly express the idea of the concrete, but the word "many" conveys the idea of the abstract. "Shed for many." "Many" is less than the whole, less than all that are *alive this day*, of this or any other nation. We may affirm of the many, what would not be true of the whole. It never was true of any nation, nor of all the individual members of all families, that the law of the Lord was put in their inward parts, and written in their hearts, nor yet that all *knew* the "Lord from the least to the greatest;" but all this may be affirmed of many, of a multitude. There were no specialties in the old covenant, and according to Jeremiah and Jesus there can be no generalities in the new covenant. "For this is my blood of the new covenant which is shed for many for the remission of sins," said Jesus, when, as yet, his blood was not shed.

When, then, may we look for this new covenant? The coincidence of time between the shedding of the paschal blood and the memorial cup of his own shed blood would suggest the next Pentecost, then near at hand, as the time of the new covenant; or when remission of sins was, for the first time offered to the house of Israel, and the house of Judah.

We will go forward about fifty days, that will bring us to the next Pentecost. The word Pentecost means the fiftieth. It was the name of a festival among the Jews, fifty days after the Passover. It was ordained by God, and was observed annually in commemoration of the giving of the law, and the fiftieth day from their departure from Egypt, which was the day after the night of the slaying of the Passover. This festival was also called the feast of weeks, because it was observed seven weeks, beginning with the 16th day of the month Nisan. This may account for the language of Acts ii., 1 : "And when the day of Pentecost was fully come, they were all with one accord in one place."

We have now come to a logical necessity. We must find the differential peculiarities of the new covenant in the historic facts of this Pentecost. We must not only find new developments here, but they must meet the prophetic and prospective specifications of Jeremiah and Jesus, else the Pentecost spoken of in Acts ii., was neither the time nor the place when the new covenant was promulgated. If there are no historic facts in the New Testament that meet the prophecy of Jeremiah, and if there is no fact that corresponds with the memorial cup, then the new covenant is yet in the future.

I affirm, then, that God made a new covenant with the house of Israel and the house of Judah on the Pentecost following the death of his Son Jesus Christ our Lord.

1. The Mediator is present. "This cup is the new covenant in my blood." (Luke xxii., 20.) This suggests that Jesus himself is the mediator. But Paul settles this question. "Now of the things we have spoken this is the sum : We have such a high-priest, who is set on the right hand of the throne of the Majesty in the heavens." "For if he were on earth he should not be a priest." "But now hath he obtained a more excellent ministry, by how much also he is (present tense) the Mediator of a better covenant, which was (past tense) established upon better promises." "For if that first covenant had been faultless, then should no place have been sought for the second." (Heb. viii., 1–6.)

The public announcements that Jesus, *the* Christ, has taken his seat on the "right hand of the Majesty in the heavens," his "priesthood," and the "new covenant," have a simultaneous beginning. These revelations date on Pentecost. (Acts ii.)

2. "Behold the days come that I will make a new covenant with the house of Israel and the house of Judah." This covenant was not to be made with Gentiles, but with Jews. "And when the day of Pentecost was fully come." "There were dwelling at Jerusalem, Jews, devout men, out of every nation under heaven." (Acts ii.) A "sound" from heaven, and an unearthly appearance of "tongues" seen upon the persons of the twelve apostles ; these strange phenomena brought this multitude of Jews together. This fact meets the prophecy. This confounded and amazed multitude were addressed. The speech contained new facts, with new motives to obey God. And its immediate result was a new order of things. "Ye men of Israel, hear these words : Jesus of Nazareth ye have taken, and by wicked hands have crucified and slain, whom God hath raised up." David, your most beloved king and prophet, foresaw this ; namely, that God of the "fruit of his loins would raise up the Messiah to sit on his throne ;" and your own David said more than this : "The Lord said unto my Lord, sit thou on my right hand until I make thy foes thy footstool."

This speech may be regarded as a vast and comprehensive predicate, from which was drawn the most transcendently glorious and overwhelming conclusion ever found in the history of logic or rhetoric. It was the first public announcement that Jesus the crucified one was *the* Christ. When Peter had confessed this fact for himself and fellow-apostles, Jesus placed them all under a solemn charge "to tell no man that he was the Christ," until he had "risen from the dead." Now the time for this revelation had expired by limitation ; still, Peter would not be first to tell the secret, but he called up David and made him tell that prejudiced nation that he whom they had crucified was their Christ. The house of Israel, and the house of Judah, from "every nation under heaven," were

represented in this great assembly. To make David a
witness for their Christ shows a depth of wisdom to which
Peter, as a man, could lay no claim. The prejudices of
many being now overcome, Peter said : "Therefore." This
was the most emphatic *therefore* ever uttered. Now, in
view of what you have seen and heard, "therefore, let all
the house of Israel know assuredly that God hath made
that same Jesus, whom ye have crucified, both Lord and
Christ." " God hath made" "both Lord and Christ," would
make a God-fearing Jew tremble. He knew the meaning
of *Lord-making*. It would call up some reminiscences. In
the excitement of the moment, they would think on the
times when God made Saul, David, and Solomon kings.
The national cry, "God save the king," rang in their ears.
" God hath made," etc., was the signal of authority to
command, and power to save.

Some things in this Pentecostal sermon were old in
prophecy, but they were all new in fact. The descent of
the Spirit, the cloven tongues, illiterate Galileans speaking all the languages of earth fluently and intelligibly, the
resurrection of Jesus, the glorification of Jesus, the announcement that he was both *the Lord* and *the Christ*, all
these were novelties of no ordinary character.

If these new and extraordinary facts, accompanied with
corresponding attestation, had produced but ordinary results, this might, or perhaps would, beget feelings of
doubt or skepticism. But if this was the time for the
promulgation of the new covenant, then these were the
facts of the new covenant, to be put into the "inward
parts," and to be written upon the hearts of those with
whom the covenant should be made.

3. " I will put my law in their inward parts, and write
it in their hearts." The following quotation from Acts ii.,
37, will show that this was effected : " Now, when they
heard this, they were pierced in their heart, and said unto
Peter and the rest of the apostles : Men and brethren,

what shall we do?" They were then deeply impressed with what they had heard. This is the figurative use of the word write—written. The sin of Judah was written "with a pen of iron upon the table of their heart." (Jer. xvii., 1.) "My son, write my commandments upon thy heart." (Prov. iii., 3.) Examples of this kind might be multiplied. Written in the heart, and pierced in their heart, are metaphors of the same import. Both mean a strong impression or conviction of the mind. The question, "Men and brethren, what shall we do?" implies strong emotion. It implies yet more, namely : That, for the present, dependence in Moses and the old covenant was ' abandoned. So long as the Jews trusted in these they would tauntingly say : We are Moses' disciples. When they accepted the apostles as religious advisers, it was a concession—a recognition that he whom they had crucified was their Messiah and Lord. "I will write my law upon their hearts." It is rare that a prophecy has been more literally fulfilled.

4. "And they shall teach no more every man his neighbor, and every man his brother, saying, Know the Lord."

Above it is said, when "they heard *this*." The antececedent to "*this*" is : "God hath made that same Jesus, whom you have crucified, both Lord and Christ." Hearing this, and believing this, produced that state of mind described by the words "pricked in their heart," and "what shall we do?" This was said of all, and therefore all knew God, from the "least to the greatest."

5. "For I will be merciful to their unrighteousness, and their sins and iniquities will I remember no more." This is the last specification in the new covenant.

We have before quoted the question proposed by these sin-convicted Jews. They knew that something was to be done, and they were ready to do it. "For new lords and new laws" is true the world over, both in heaven and on earth. How shall we recognize the supremacy of him whom God has constituted "both Lord and Christ,"—what shall we do? "Repent and be baptized, every one of you, in the name of Jesus Christ, for the remission of sins, and you shall receive the gift of the Holy Spirit." This was the answer to the question, What shall we do? Now the new covenant, in all its specialties and differential phases, was submitted to "the house of Israel and the house of Judah." If accepted, the new covenant was made, and the prophecy, "for I will be merciful to their unrighteousness, and their sins and iniquities will I remember no more," was now fulfilled. The question now is on the acceptance.

"Then they that gladly received his word were baptized ; and the same day there were added unto them about three thousand souls." This was a formal acceptance, and the new covenant was now a fact. For this we have higher authority than inference. Jesus, *the* Christ, associated the existence of the new covenant with the shedding of his blood. If the new covenant is not yet, the Lord's Supper commemorates a falsehood. For every time the minister says : "This cup is the new covenant in my blood, which is shed for you," he says what is not true. Again : Paul, himself a Jew, and well acquainted with the prophetical writings, and under plenary inspiration, has associated the glorification of Christ, his priesthood, his mediatorship of the new covenant, and the vanishing away of the old covenant in the same order of time. (Heb. viii.)

We do then reaffirm, without the fear of honorable criticism, that God did make the new covenant on the Pentecost, *the last "fiftieth"* of the Mosaic Dispensation. That we have the record of this stupendous work, the overflowing of this immeasurable favor and love to a ruined world in the second chapter of the Acts of Apostles.

There remains yet another important phase of the subject. Did God make this covenant with all Israel, as he did in Horeb, or with individuals ? The answer must be :

No. Not even with all that were assembled on the occasion, for some of the multitude mocked, and said the apostles were drunken. Who then? Those who "heard" —were "pricked in their hearts"—asked, "What shall we do?" And yet more definitely, "Be baptized, every one of you," individually, on your own responsibility. The covenant of circumcision and the covenant of Horeb had universality, where the new covenant has individuality. The doors of these covenants are hung on different hinges. Faith will make a better hinge than flesh, for it is better material. Still, faith is exceedingly ductile—it may be drawn out to great length. Where there is an understanding head and an impressible heart there may be faith.

Let no one charge the new covenant with narrowness. "For the promise" (of these covenanted mercies) "is unto you and your children, and to all that are afar off, *even* as many as the Lord our God shall call." "And I will be to them a God, and they shall be to me a people," is also a promise of the new covenant.

The new covenant called out a new people for the Lord. It made a new classification of humanity. Before this the classification was "the circumcision" and the "uncircumcision," or Jew and Gentile. But after the new covenant was inaugurated the classification was "Jew" and "Gentile," and "the Church of God." "And the Lord added to the church daily the saved." (Acts ii., 47.) This is the first time the word church is applied to an organized society. The word church occurs in Mat. xvi. : "And upon this rock will I build my church." "Will I build my church" is in the future tense. The Church of God at this time existed in design, not in fact. The word church occurs once more in Mat. xviii. : "Tell it to the church." Here the word church must have been used in a prospective sense, for there is nothing between the sixteenth and the eighteenth chapters of Matthew that looks like church *building*. This view is confirmed by the fact that the word church is used but twice in Matthew, and then in the future tense ; and not once does the word church occur in Mark, Luke, or John. Why should the last three evangelists have ignored the institution if it did exist in the days of the Messiah ? This silence can be explained only on the supposition that Christ had not yet built his church.

In making the new covenant, Jesus Christ made for himself a new church—"people," to use the language of Jeremiah. Indeed, a church without a covenant would be as anomalous as a sect without a creed, or a government without a constitution. The church which originated on the day of Pentecost constituted God's "people," and he was their covenant God.

Dr. Adam Clarke spoke well on this subject. (See his Commentary, preface to Acts.) "In the book of Acts, we see how the Church of Christ was formed and settled." "As far as any church can show that it has followed this model, so far it is holy and apostolic." The prophecy of Jeremiah, before cited in full, is given in detail. And in its fullest detail it is found in the second chapter of Acts. Thus far we have looked at the new covenant through the eye of prophecy, henceforth we shall look at it through the eye of history.

The converts on the day of Pentecost stand in a different relation to the new covenant and the church from all others, whether Jews or Gentiles. With these the new covenant was made, and these were the material of which Christ formed his church, his body, his temple. These were the original covenantees. All subsequent converts were additions. A covenant must exist before parties can be taken into it ; a church must be formed before members can be added ; hence, the first time the word "church" occurs as a descriptive noun we have the word "added." "And the Lord added to the church daily." To be in the covenant is to be in the church, and *vice versa*. But as yet no Gentile was taken into covenant with God. They were still "without Christ," "aliens," "strangers from the covenants of promise." They had no "hope," and were "without God in the world." The Gentiles being left out up to this date was not an oversight on the part of God ; and when admitted it was not a new thing in the divine purpose.

As we have seen in the first formal statement of the new covenant, the Gentiles were embraced in common with the unconverted Jews. "For the promise is to you, and to your children, and to all that are afar off, even as many as the Lord our God shall call." (Acts ii., 39.) "Afar off" always refers to the Gentiles. Again : "Ye are the children of the prophets, and of the covenant God made with our fathers, saying unto Abraham, And in thy seed shall all the kindreds of the earth be blessed. Unto you first," etc. (Acts iii., 25.) And again : "Go preach the gospel to every creature." (Mark xvi., 15.)

The next thing in the order of narrative is the calling of the Gentiles. We will now turn to the tenth chapter of Acts. Cornelius, a centurion and a Gentile, was the first upon whom this honor and grace were bestowed. He was "a devout man, and one that feared God with all his house, who gave much alms to the people, and prayed to God always." He "saw in a vision" "an angel," "saying," "Cornelius," "now send men to Joppa, and call for one Simon Peter." "He lodgeth with one Simon, a tanner," "he shall tell thee what thou oughtest to do." "Immediately, therefore, I sent to thee (Peter), and thou hast well done that thou hast come. Now, therefore, we are all here present before God, to hear all things that are commanded thee of God." "Then Peter opened his mouth," and stated the same facts concerning Jesus *the* Christ he had stated eight years before in the city of Jerusalem, on the day of Pentecost. When he had stated the last specification of the new covenant, namely, "remission of sins," the speaker was interrupted by the descent of the Spirit. He had now gone far enough in his statement for the present, and the Lord arrested him quickly. "To him give all the prophets witness that through his name whosoever believeth in him shall receive remission of sins. While Peter yet spake these words, the Holy Spirit fell on all them which heard the word. And they of the circumcision which believed were astonished, as many as came with Peter, because that on the Gentiles also was poured out the gift of the Holy Ghost. For they heard them speak with tongues, and magnify God. Then answered Peter, Can any man forbid water that these should not be baptized, who have received the Holy Ghost as well as we? And he commanded them to be baptized in the name of the Lord."

Now the new covenant was proposed and accepted by Gentiles. This opened the door for their acceptance. From this time the Gentiles had a covenant, they had promise, they had hope, and they had God in the world. But here, not as the covenant of circumcision made with Abraham, nor the old covenant made at Horeb, but as the new covenant made with Jews on the Pentecost.

The first two covenants took the entire mass of "flesh," all that were "alive" at the time of covenanting; but this did not embrace all the Gentiles *en masse.* There was a limitation. That limitation is expressed in the two following words, "whosoever believeth." This gracious covenant is open to the acceptance of every believing Gentile. "Whosoever believeth" is making an exception, and exceptions make rules. Every believing Gentile comes under the rule. He may become a party to the covenant, as the believing Cornelius and the believing members of his household did; for if there were members in the family of this Gentile that did not believe, the same rule that accepted him would exclude them. "To Him give all the prophets witness, that through his name *whosoever believeth in him* shall receive remission of sins." We shall next call attention to the moral effects of this gracious visitation. To do this with profit we must first know the moral condition of the Gentiles before the gospel was preached to them. Read again : " Wherefore remember, that ye *being* in time past Gentiles in the flesh, who are called uncircumcision by that which is called *the* circumcision in the flesh made by hands. That at that time ye were without Christ, being aliens from the commonwealth of Israel, and strangers from the covenants of promise, having no hope, and without God in the world." This describes a national distinction. That distinction originated in the word of God to Abraham : " My covenant shall be in your flesh." The line of demarkation was neither faith nor piety, but flesh—circumcised and uncircumcised flesh. This was not an imaginary, but a real line, drawn by the hand of God for aims and objects most appreciable, of which we can not now speak.

All the descendants of Abraham, through Isaac and Jacob, were on one side. These, as we have before stated, had covenants, promises, hope, and God. The Gentiles had neither covenant, promise, nor hope ; hence my text says they were " without God in the world." In the national sense of these promises, what applied to one Jew applied to every Jew, as respects "this world ;" and what applied to one Gentile applied to every Gentile, as respects this world. The pious Cornelius was, therefore, in the same condition, as respects divine recognition, that all other Gentiles were—" without hope, and without God in the world." Some will say that is in contradiction with his character. It is not character, but state or condition, that belongs to this discussion. The condition of Cornelius is as truly, by every rule of interpretation, involved in the text, " without hope, and without God in the world," as is that of the most profligate Gentile. But you anticipate. Can a " devout," " God-fearing," " benevolent," " prayer-

ful" man be "without hope, and without God in the
world?" This was possible in the time of which Paul
speaks, for he says: "At that time ye were without
Christ," etc., but this would not be possible now with
individuals or communities favored with the gospel as we
are.

But there was yet something for Cornelius to do before
he could be enfranchised with gospel honors and blessings,
as we shall see. Send for "Peter, he shall tell thee what
thou oughtest to do." (Acts x., 5, 6.) Peter, in self-defense,
states the instruction to Cornelius in this form: "Who
shall tell thee words, whereby thou and all thy house shall
be saved." (Acts xi., 14.) The apostle found this good
man unsaved in the sense of remission of sins, and left him
a saved Gentile—a sinner saved. The words spoken, by
which these first-fruits of the Gentiles were brought into
covenant with God, are recorded in the tenth chapter of
Acts. Every Gentile can, and should, examine the record
for himself. This was a national tender of the gospel,
with all its promises and hopes; but the acceptance of it
was then, is now, and ever will be, personal. "And he
commanded them to be baptized in the name of the Lord."

Paul follows the words of my text, and says for the con-
solation of the Gentile converts in the church at Ephesus:
"Now, therefore, ye are no more strangers and foreigners,
but fellow-citizens with the saints, and of the household of
God; and are built upon the foundation of the apostles
and prophets, Jesus Christ himself being the chief corner-
stone: in whom all the building, fitly framed together,
groweth into a holy temple of the Lord; in whom ye
(Gentiles) are builded together, for a habitation of God
through the Spirit." (Eph. ii.)

If the "prophets" here named had been the Old Testament prophets, the order of statement would have been
prophets and apostles. If the prophets were the *Jewish*,
there is a mistake in the classification. "He ascended,"

"And he gave some apostles and some prophets," etc., "for the edifying of the body of Christ." The church rests upon a New Testament basis. Jesus Christ, whatever his relations were to the church in the wilderness, was not the "chief corner-stone." Moreover, the apostles and prophets, the builders, were New Testament officials. Both Jews and Gentiles were built together, for a habitation of God through the Spirit—this is his dwelling-place on earth. But for this, the world would be a God-forsaken world.

This union, for this object, is the "Lord's doing, and we behold it with admiration." Paul speaks of two mysteries. One is : "God manifest in the flesh," "preached unto the Gentiles," and "received up into glory." And the other mystery is, that the Gentiles should be "fellow-heirs with the Jews, and of the same body, and partakers of the promise in Christ by the gospel." This, too, he calls the unsearchable riches of Christ. "Unto me, who am less than the least of all saints, is this grace given, that I should preach among the Gentiles the unsearchable riches of Christ ; and to make all men see what is the fellowship of the mystery," etc.

"The fellowship of the mystery," the union of Jews and Gentiles in one body, is a *mysterious fellowship*, hitherto kept secret. When we take into account how difficult it is to reconcile and unite contending parties, even when both confess, and mutually acknowledge each other to be Christians, then is this mystery greatly enhanced. The animosity between Jews and Gentiles was of long standing. Their prejudices were bitter, and their hatred was cruel. But under the light, purity, and sympathy of the gospel, they forgot their old differences, and "loved as brethren." The union was not a compromise, but a real settlement of difficulties. When Peter returned from Cesarea to Jerusalem, after his visit to Cornelius, the church preferred a charge against him : "Thou wentest in to men uncircumcised, and didst eat with them." The last words in his defense were the following : "What was I, that I could withstand God?" "When they heard these things they held their peace and glorified God, saying, Then hath God also to the Gentiles granted repentance unto life." And everywhere the salvation of the Gentiles was cause of grateful rejoicing among the Jewish converts for a time. But it could scarcely be expected that this work of reconciling and uniting would be permitted to go on without some interruption. It was interrupted, but not on account of personal, but doctrinal differences.

The history of these troubles, and the final disposition of them, we have in the fifteenth chapter of Acts. When Paul and Barnabas were laboring in Antioch, a Gentile city, certain men who came down from Judea taught the brethren, and said : "Except ye be circumcised after the manner of Moses, ye can not be saved." This was an issue, and some discussion followed. These parties determined that Paul and Barnabas should go to Jerusalem, and the question should be referred to the apostles and elders. And on their way they declared the conversion of the Gentiles, and caused great joy. Being now received by the church, "there rose up certain of the sect of the Phari-sees, which believed, saying, "that it was needful to cir-cumcise them (the Gentiles), and command them to keep the law of Moses." Before we proceed further with this history, let us inquire into the probable motive.

If circumcision and the law had been enforced by the apostles, there would have been no occasion for this now ; therefore circumcision, as a condition of salvation, only served to conceal the real motive. The believing Phari-sees in Jerusalem were better logicians. They saw clearly that circumcision could not be imposed upon the Gentiles, only by means of the law. Salvation could not have been the object of this requisition, for salvation never was a promise of circumcision or the law of Moses ; therefore much less could they be conditions of salvation now.

Neither was there any thing lovely in the rite of circumcision that would have made its continuance desirable.

Perhaps we shall find the real motive of these early Judaizers in the original design of circumcision. "And my covenant shall be in your flesh for an everlasting covenant." This, doubtless, explains the reason for this appendage to the gospel. Whatever was the disposing motive of one Judaizer was the motive of all Judaizers, whether at Antioch, Jerusalem, or Galatia. Paul, a Jew, will be good authority on this question. He says : "For neither they themselves who are circumcised keep the law ; but desire to have you (Gentiles) circumcised, that they may glory in your flesh." (Gal. vi., 13.) We shall collate a few passages bearing on this point. "If any other man thinketh that he hath whereof he might trust in the flesh, I more : Circumcised the eighth day, of the stock of Israel, of the tribe of Benjamin, an Hebrew of the Hebrews." (Phil. iii., 4, 5.) In the third verse of the same chapter : "For we worship God in the Spirit, and have no confidence in the flesh." This implies that some had "confidence in the flesh." The Judaizing teachers, then, "had confidence in the flesh." They "trusted in the flesh." "They gloried in the flesh." They were flesh-proud. Gentile flesh was uncircumcised flesh. The Gentile had no covenant in his flesh, therefore these Jewish Christians looked upon their Gentile brethren as unclean. But this was not the worst of the case, for the gospel had nothing that came in the room of circumcision, and the Gentiles being received without it, it was a legitimate inference that according to the Christian religion there was no such thing as sanctified flesh entitled to special divine favor ; hence the dogma, "except ye be circumcised after the manner of Moses ye can not be saved."

"And the apostles and elders came together for to consider of this matter ; and when there had been much disputing, Peter rose up and said." He then gave a synopsis of his visit to Cornelius, and drew from these premises two conclusions :

1. "Now, therefore, why tempt ye God to put a yoke upon the neck of the disciples, which neither our fathers nor we were able to bear." This yoke was what his opponents contended for—circumcision and the law of Moses.

2. "But we believe, that through the grace of the Lord Jesus Christ we shall be saved *even* as they."

The logic of this conclusion is not seen at first view. The Jews had priority. Then why did he not state it thus : they (the Gentiles) shall be saved as we (the Jews). This form of statement would have been construed in favor of the affirmants. For as they always had and were then observing circumcision and the law, therefore the same should be required of the Gentiles. But as God had accepted and saved the Gentiles by grace, without circumcision and the law, therefore "we shall be saved even as they." That is, without circumcision and the law of Moses. This form of his conclusion made the means by which the Gentiles were saved, the rule and the standard, and the Jews had to conform to that. This was a logical thunderbolt. The word "saved" was here used in its most current sense, in the sense of pardon. And as the argument had a national bearing, the future tense was the right tense. Moreover, the eternal salvation is not usually, if ever, ascribed to grace.

Then all the multitude kept silence and gave audience to Barnabas and Paul, declaring what miracles and wonders God had wrought among the Gentiles by them. These "miracles and wonders" are indications of God's purpose to save the Gentiles without "circumcision and the law of Moses." This would be the legitimate conclusion.

"And after they held their peace, James answered, saying, Men and brethren hearken unto me : Simon hath declared how God at the first did visit the Gentiles to take out of them a people for his name." And to this agree the words of the prophets, as it is written : "After this I will return and will build again the tabernacle of David which is fallen down, and I will build again the ruins thereof, · and I will set it up. That the residue of men might seek after the Lord, and all the Gentiles upon whom my name is called, saith the Lord, who doeth all these things." (Amos ix., 11, 12.) "Known unto God are all his works from the beginning of the world." These are the premises from which James gave his final decision.

We must have definite views of his argument before we can see the fitness of his conclusions. There are three facts in the apostle's argument : 1. The calling of the Gentiles. 2. The rebuilding of the tabernacle of David. 3. The falling down of the tabernacle of David.

In stating categories we sometimes state the first last and the last first. So here, these events in their order of time were : 1. The tabernacle of David fell down. 2. It was set up again. 3. The Gentiles were called. This falling down and setting up was, "that the residue of men · might seek after the Lord." This stands as the consequence or result. This corresponds exactly with the establishment and progress of the gospel. The old covenant, with its order of things, was abrogated. The new covenant, and what pertains to it, was established. The Gentiles were called and saved by the grace of God, and circumcision and the law of Moses had not been commanded to either Jew or Gentile. This would be understood by that audience, and the bearing upon the question at issue, "Except ye be circumcised and keep the law of Moses ye can not be saved," would be seen.

This breaking down and building up and visiting the Gentiles that they might seek after the Lord, that the Lord might "take out from among them a people for his name," are things that the Lord had done as a means to an end. "That the residue of men might seek after the Lord, and all the Gentiles upon whom my name is called, saith the Lord, who doeth all these things ; known unto God are

2*

all his works from the beginning of the world." The bearing of this last sentence must not be overlooked. That the tabernacle of David should fall down, that it should be built again, that the Gentiles should hear the gospel and believe, were things known of God from the beginning of the world. Predestined that they should be as means to an end in human redemption. For fifteen hundred years the children of Abraham, according to the flesh, were his only and peculiar people. They still had the privilege of being his people, but not exclusively so. And the residue of men had no mediator, no covenant, no promise. They had no tabernacle ; they were left to themselves, "to walk in their own ways." But when God determined to take from these nations hitherto passed by "a people for his name," he determined to make for them a new tabernacle. For this there was a necessity, "that the residue of men might seek after the Lord." The implication is, that this "residue" would not have sought the Lord in the old tabernacle, of which we shall have more to say at another place.

Wherefore my sentence is, that we "trouble not them which from among the Gentiles have turned to God." Simon has said, that circumcision and the law of Moses was an oppressive yoke. This would be so to the Gentiles, and without any profit. Then James proceeded with his sentence : "But that we will write unto them, that they abstain from the pollutions of idols, and from fornication, and from things strangled, and from blood." This looks like some concession to the believing Pharisees. And what follows ? A reason for this concession : "For Moses of old time hath in every city them that preach him, being read in the synagogues every Sabbath day." This was conciliatory, but it was no compromise. Idolatry and fornication were immoralities, as contrary to the gospel as they were to the law. And eating flesh without blood-letting was forbidden. by God in the covenant with Noah : "But the flesh, with the life thereof, which is the blood thereof, shall ye not eat."

(Gen. ix., 4.) Strangulation was the easiest way of taking the life of an animal, and retain the blood in the flesh; therefore practiced by the Gentiles, and when the blood was let it was usually eaten by them. This prohibition was not originally Mosaic, but patriarchal. It was therefore a law to mankind, as universal in its application as the law that forbids murder. (Gen. ix., 6.) To recommend to the Gentile converts to abstain from things strangled, and from blood, was not to enjoin upon them a Jewish ceremonial, as the prohibition antedates the Mosaic law. But this seeming concession had some important bearings upon the issue:

1. It would suggest to the believing Pharisees, that the opposition to Moses and the law was not a prejudice against either.

2. In its social bearings it was all important; for as the Jewish brethren had conscientious scruples about eating things strangled, and blood, and the Gentiles had long indulged in this habit, it would greatly mar their social intercourse. This concession would promote more intimacy between the Jewish and Gentile converts, and bring them on better terms.

3. As we have said in another place, exceptions make rules. "For it seemed good to the Holy Spirit and to us, that we lay upon you no greater burden than these necessary things. That ye (Gentiles) abstain from meats offered to idols, and from blood, and from things strangled, and from fornication, from which if ye keep yourselves ye shall do well. Fare ye well."

These four things commanded by Moses in the law were enjoined upon the Gentile Christians, while circumcision and every other commandment of the law were excluded, as not coming under the rule adopted by the Holy Spirit, the apostles, and elders.

The Pharisees did not contend for the law in some abstract sense. Moral, judicial, ceremonial, is a modern human classification of the law. The Pharisees affirmed that it was needful to circumcise them, and to command them to keep the law of Moses. By the law of Moses they meant the whole law given by Moses. The apostles and elders, under the guidance of inspiration, so understood the question in debate; therefore these four things commanded by Moses in the law come under the rule for Gentile observance, by which decision they were exonerated from circumcision, and the hundred and one other things commanded in the law of Moses, further than as the precepts of Moses were modified and incorporated with the law of Christ. As for example, Jesus said to his disciples: "Moses said, thou shalt not kill;" but I say you shall not indulge the passion that would prompt the act, and to cherish impure desire is adultery, and hatred is murder. (See Matt. v., and 1 John iii., 15.) The precepts so modified are now received as Christian doctrine, not as commanded by Moses, but by Jesus Christ.

We shall now return to a more critical examination of the "tabernacle." We must get into the interior. If the tabernacle of David represents the old covenant order of things when rebuilt, "set up again," does it not concede to Pedobaptists that the Church of Christ is but a continuation of the Jewish Church? Whether this is so or not will depend: 1. Upon the meaning of the word "tabernacle." 2. The object the apostle had for bringing this prophecy of Amos before the convention. 3. The application to the question under discussion.

"Skeene, a tent, tabernacle, that is, generally, any temporary dwelling," etc.; "a house, that is, tropically, a family, lineage, roll." (Acts xv., 16, Greenfield's Lexicon.) According to this authority, the word tabernacle is used in some ten different senses in the Scriptures. We may, then, substitute that definition which agrees best with the general scope of the subject. If the controversy had been in regard to the lineal descent of the Messiah, the word "tabernacle" might be understood only in that limited sense. But as that was not the issue, it must be understood in a more extended sense. Shall the Gentiles be commanded to circumcise their children, and keep the law of Moses, was the issue. For the settlement of this question, the Apostle James appealed to the Prophet Amos. And his application of the prophecy to the question in debate is found in the words of his final "sentence" briefly expressed. My sentence is, that we "trouble not the Gentiles" with "circumcision," and the "law of Moses." The trouble of certain believing Jews was in regard to the reconstruction of the tabernacle. There were some things in the old tabernacle which had fallen down, which had been left out of the new tabernacle, as now set up. Circumcision and the law of Moses had been left out, and they wanted to get them in. This was their only complaint. The tabernacle, then, which had fallen down, meant the Jewish order of things ; and the tabernacle as now rebuilt, the Christian order of things. "This tabernacle," says Paul, "the Lord pitched, and not man." With propriety, when set up again, it was still called the tabernacle of David, for the Lord that "pitched" this true tabernacle was David's Son and successor. Things, persons, and institutions may be called by the same name, and be neither identical nor similar. Indeed, the very idea that the new would be like the old is preposterous. The old, said the prophet, is fallen down. It was not a good house, or it would not have "fallen down." It must have been deficient in its mechanism or material. There was too much flesh in it to make a permanent dwelling-place for the Lord and his people. And as we have before hinted, literal circumcision has respect to flesh. This being left out of the tabernacle, as reconstructed by David's Son, has been the cause of all the Judaizing both ancient and modern ; therefore the effort in the days of the apostles to get circumcision admitted into the new covenant, and since then to find a substitute for it.

Perhaps nothing has been so much wrested and perverted as the words, "My covenant shall be in your flesh;" and nothing in religion has so much tenacity of life. The words of our Lord, "This cup is the new covenant in my blood which is shed for you," have been held with a feeble grasp compared with this. Does not the assumption that baptism has come in the room of circumcision go on the supposition that God's covenant is still in the flesh of believing parents? The use Pedobaptists make of the few household baptisms recorded in the New Testament looks in the same direction. When the Holy Spirit, apostles, and elders had given a prompt denial to circumcision and sanctified flesh, these were quickened into life again under another form. There must be some powerful, active motive underlying the idea of transferable grace in the flesh. Without this the Papacy would cease to be. She would have to abandon the name Catholic (general), the universal church. Like Judaism, she takes the aggregate, all the living, into her covenant. The same is true of every State establishment. The State religion of Scotland was, at least in part, gotten up by State agents. It required the wisest men of the nation *five* years to make the Confession of Faith, and then they had to call in the aid of Parliament. Suppose there were no dissenters in England, her commonwealth and her church would be the same numerically as was the Jewish nation and church, and by the same instrumentality a "covenant in the flesh;" for if the infant offspring of church members only are entitled to baptism, this exclusive privilege must be based upon the flesh of the parents, or upon the flesh of the offspring, or upon the flesh of both. Either this special grace is on account of the begetter or the begotten. If on account of the begetter, then religious privileges and gospel blessings are communicated by flesh to flesh. Then the blessings of the new covenant rest upon the same old covenant basis. This is the Pedobaptist predicate. Hence the long and labored effort to maintain the identity of the covenants and the church. Therefore Pedobaptists take in the aggregate by baptism as Abraham did by circumcision, and ignore all the specialties of the new covenant. If circumcision had been based upon individual faith, the Jewish church would have been less than the Jewish commonwealth (State), as the believers would have been few compared with those who would not, and others who could not, believe. The religious and political nationality resting upon the same fleshy basis, made the one just as broad as the other. The Jewish church was the Jewish world, and the Jewish world was the Jewish church.

This question was so understood by Jesus Christ when he said to the twelve apostles : "Ye are not of the world, but I have chosen you out of the world." The church that then was. (John xv., 19.)

All Pedobaptist churches retain this Jewish feature, for they give as many subjects to the State as they have members in their respective bodies.

But upon this question of "flesh" we should say more. A sentiment that attaches so much sacredness and is so deeply rooted is not easily eradicated, nor *even* shown to be a fallacy. In this case, as in all religious error, the error is but a truth perverted to subserve a purpose, or innocently misunderstood. The truth is, that God did sanctify the flesh of Abraham. He did for a time appropriate it to his own use ; and upon this consecration he based covenanted promises. God did respect this flesh, so long as it was of any use to him in the accomplishment of his purposes. When his Son had come in the flesh, had died in the flesh, had rose again in the flesh, the object was accomplished. "Wherefore henceforth know we no man on account of the flesh : yea, though we have known Christ after the flesh, yet now henceforth know we him no more." (See 2 Cor. v., 14–17.) The mortal flesh of the Son of God descended through a long line of sanctified flesh. He was therefore entitled to respect on this account. But when he had accomplished his work in the flesh, Paul says, we respect him no more on account of the flesh.

Again : "For if the blood of bulls," etc., "sanctifieth to the purifying of the flesh : how much more shall the blood of Christ purge your conscience from dead works to serve the living God." (Heb. ix., 13, 14.)

The error of the Jews consisted in making a substance of shadows, and realities of types. They attached holy qualities to flesh. They might with equal propriety have assigned holy qualities to an altar of earth or stone, to gold or silver, the temple and all its furniture, as to their flesh : for all these the law declared sanctified. But all these were only set apart from a common to a special use, as was circumcised sanctified flesh. The holy qualities of the heart were by the Judaizers transferred to the flesh. This fatal error pervaded the Jewish mind in the days of Jesus Christ and his apostles. The current belief was, to eat with unwashed hands, cups, pots, tables, or unclean food, defiled the man. But Jesus said to them, Not these, but that which "cometh out of the man." "For from within, out of the heart of men, proceed evil thoughts, adulteries, covetousness, pride, foolishness. All these evil things come from within, and defile the man." (Mark vii., 20–22.)

In answer to the same delusion, Jesus said to Nicodemus : "That which is born of flesh, is flesh." Faith and piety are no more born of the flesh than angels and spirits. That master in Israel should have known this, and until he did he could neither understand nor appreciate the new birth. On another occasion Jesus said to the flesh-proud Jews : "The flesh profiteth nothing." (John vi., 63.) "For I know that in me, that is in my flesh, dwelleth no good thing." (Rom. vii., 18.) John the Baptist rebuked the same ruinous error, when he said to the Pharisees and Sadducees : "And think not to say within yourselves, we have Abraham to our father," etc. John anticipated these religionists. He knew they thought to claim his baptism, because they were the children of Abraham according to the flesh, and not on the condition of repentance.

"Except ye be circumcised after the manner of Moses, ye can not be saved," was but the odor of the old cask. It was the cause of more controversy in New Testament times than all other questions taken together. What it was among the early Jewish converts it has been among Gentile Christians. It has been, and yet is, a disturbing element. The cause of more controversy among professing Christians than all other religious differences in the aggregate. Its influence upon the church now is what it was in the apostolic age,—dissension and strife. In the days of the apostles the controversy originated in a persistent effort to bring into the new covenant things that belonged to the old abrogated covenant. This is precisely the issue between the advocates of infant and believers' baptism. The former maintain that baptism is a "sign and a seal of the covenant of grace," and its promised blessings; some of the latter maintain that baptism is the formal acceptance of the new covenant, and its promised blessings are realities to the baptized. But there is another issue underlying this, which may be stated briefly; thus, faith and flesh right, and faith right only. The history of the controversy suggests that the parties regard the question as one of great merit. That it is not an empty puerility, in this they agree. In this they must agree, or there could be no cause for disagreement. Would it not be foolish to have controversy of a thousand years' continuance about a non-essential; and to write more books about a thing of no importance than the world can contain? The admitted importance *only* can justify the controversial attention bestowed upon the subject. The lucid fact is, that this question, like its exact prototype, involves the calling and salvation of the Gentiles as truly and almost identically as the question which originated at Antioch, and was referred to the apostles for decision. The question then was not, whether God had or had not called the Gentiles ; but the question turned upon the "how" it was or should be done. "Except ye (Gentiles) be circumcised ye can not be saved," was raising a question of means to an end. Now we have the question in a nutshell. "Simon hath declared," said James, "how God at the first did visit the Gentiles, to take out of them a people for his name." "How God at the first," etc. The first meaning of the word "how," is "in what manner." We will now substitute this definition. This is an admissible rule of interpretation, and an end of all strife. "Simon has declared in what manner God at the first." Peter in his speech before the convention referred to the incidents recorded in Acts x. From these he stated three :

1. "God made choice among us, that the Gentiles by my mouth should hear the word of the gospel and believe."

2. "And God, which knoweth the hearts, bear them witness (of acceptance), giving them the Holy Ghost, even as *he did* unto us."

3. "And put no difference between us and them, purifying their hearts by faith." The witness-bearing had a ·national meaning, and was not repeated since the conversion of Cornelius. Now this is the sum : "Preaching," "hearing," "believing," "purifying the heart by faith." To these he adds, through "grace" they were "saved." This much Peter said, in the meeting on the "how" the first Gentiles were called and saved. Then in the prophecy of Amos, cited by James, we have one thing more that belongs to the "how," "and all the Gentiles upon whom my name is called, saith the Lord, who doeth all these things."

"And all the Gentiles upon whom my name is called." What can this mean ? It is not prayer. For then *we* call upon the name of the Lord in the first person, but "upon whom my name is called" involves the idea of a second person,—the person calling the name of the Lord, and the person upon whom the name of the Lord is called ; evidently this is an allusion to the baptismal formula, for nothing else will meet this part of the prophecy of Amos. In the calling of the Gentiles, the last things said or done by Peter are the following : "Through his name whosoever believeth in him shall receive remission of sins." "And he commanded them to be baptized in the name of the Lord." (Acts x., 43–48.) "Teach all nations, baptizing them into the name of the Father, and of the Son, and of the Holy Ghost." Therefore, all the converts, whether Jews or Gentiles, were baptized in the name of the Lord.

One part of the prophecy of Amos relates to baptism, as one of the "things" the Lord would do "to take out of the Gentiles a people for his name." Circumcision and the law of Moses do not belong to the "how," the manner, in which God sorted out of the Gentiles a "people" for himself. "To take out of them," suggests a sorting, grading, selecting process. This corresponds with the specialties of the new covenant, as we have before shown. God did not take out of the Jews a people for his name, until the Pentecost in the second chapter of Acts. And then only those upon whom his name—the name of the Lord—was called. "Repent and be baptized, every one of you, in the name of the Lord Jesus, for the remission of sins."

Now the Lord was taking out of his own people, a people for his name. His former people, under the old covenant, were not "taken out," were not selected, but taken in the aggregate, not one was excluded or left out of the number. The process is thus described : "In the self-same day was Abraham circumcised, and Ishmael his son, and all the men of his house." (Gen. xvii., 26.) Again : The Lord "made" this "covenant" with "all of us who are here alive this day." (Deut. v., 2.) This was the process of formation, of covenanting.

In the new covenant there is a strong element of exclusiveness. Language can not express this thought with more energy than the phrase "take out of." The same peculiarity is expressed by the words "upon whom my

name is called." This "calling" the name of the Lord
" upon," is not a lawless affair. The believing penitent is
the only Scripture-qualified subject of this invocation.
There is but one thing under heaven that men are author-
ized to do in the name of the Father, Son, and Holy Spirit,
and that is to administer and receive the ordinance of
baptism. And believers only are the subjects of this
administration. The gospel is therefore, necessarily,
strongly impressed with the idea of exclusiveness, but
without the charge of partiality or favoritism. For to one
large class of humanity the gospel can be of no immediate
avail ; and to another, the tender of the gospel would only
be to cast heaven's most precious pearls before swine.
The work of converting sinners to God is a "taking out"—
a calling out. In this, Universalists excepted, there is
agreement among all professions. For even Pedobaptists
take only believers and their infants out of the whole
aggregate, and exclude all others. There is yet another
point of agreement, namely, That baptism consisting in a
formula of words spoken, and an action performed, has an
intimate relation to the new covenant. There may be a
difference of opinion as to what that relation is, but in the
fact all agree.

We shall now more critically examine the Pedobaptist
relation of baptism to the new covenant, and then the
Scriptural relation. Their doctrinal standards say "baptism
is a sign and a seal of the covenant of grace, of ingrafting
into Christ of remission of sins," etc. The words "sign"
and "seal" express the relation. That meddlesome thing
we call curiosity, is tempted to inquire : Where did the
words "sign" and "seal" come from? They are not in any
Scriptural connection with baptism. They are not a Pedobaptist invention, for that would contradict that philoso-
phy which denies to the human mind creative powers.
"Sign" and "seal" are borrowed from Abraham and circumcision. "And he received the sign of circumcision—a

seal of the righteousness of the faith which *he had yet* being uncircumcised." (Rom. iv., 11.) This *draft* goes upon the assumption that baptism came in the room of circumcision. The "Holy Spirit" is the Christian "seal." "Sealed with that Holy Spirit of promise." (Eph. i., 13.) If baptism is also a "seal," then the new covenant has two seals to attest its authenticity. We have done with the word "seal."

There are two things in a sign—visibility and invisibility. So understood by the advocates of infant baptism, hence they say: "Baptism is an outward sign of inward, spiritual grace." Circumcision was indeed a visible sign to all who received it—a sign that they were of the flesh of Abraham. But it was to Abraham at the time he received it an outward sign of an invisible faith he had in God. The sign of foul weather appears in fair weather. The sign over the artist's or merchant's door is outward and visible, because the artist and the goods are inward and invisible. The thing signified is not where the sign is. If it were the sign would be of no use. When the merchant removes his merchandise to another place he takes away his sign, else his sign would be a deception. If baptism administered to an infant is a "sign of the covenant of grace," and its promised blessings, what is it in case of incorrigible wickedness at the end of one's life? Is not the "sign" a deception? The same difficulty will arise in the case of believers' baptism, for it sometimes so happens that baptized believers do return to their wallowing again in the mire. In that case, when the reality is not, or has ceased, is the sign taken away. But this baptismal "sign" is clearly a fallacy. For it can only in any case be a "sign," either to the receiver or the beholder, during the moment of its administration. So soon as the baptismal waters have evaporated, the sign is gone. Whether a philosopher would weep or smile at such logic, I presume not to say.

In the light of the gospel, baptism is a reality. This proposition only needs statement, not argument. When the three thousand on the day of Pentecost "gladly received the word and were baptized," was not the promise of remission of sins and the gift of the Holy Spirit a present reality. When the formula "in the name of the Lord Jesus" was pronounced upon them, were they not immediately "taken out of," etc., "to be a people for the Lord?" The same is true in the case of Cornelius and his believing household. When they were baptized in the name of the Lord they were "taken out." They had more than "a sign" of the new covenant—they were parties in the new covenant. They were no more of the outside Gentile world, but they belonged to the Church of God. The gospel and its spiritual blessings were an immediate gracious realization.

The Jews made realities of shadows, and Pedobaptists make a "sign" a mere shadow, out of a reality. By this means the ordinance of baptism has been greatly depreciated. In the Protestant markets it is now offered, and taken at a large discount, while a few hold it at *par*. And for this they are stamped with an odious peculiarity, are denied the honor of being either evangelical or orthodox. If this long, expensive, and vexed controversy is legitimate, the divine teachings are seriously involved. Either the Scriptures are self-contradictory, or the language so equivocal that they can scarcely be trusted on any question of of truth and duty. This controversy, and the consequences growing out of it, are a great reproach to the church, and by association Jesus Christ is made to share the reproach, and justly, if his laws are so wanting in perspicacity, that some base the right of induction upon flesh, others, upon faith ; what some call but a sign, others regard as present reality.

But, thanks be to the Lord, all these troubles were provided for. In A. D. 52, originated the first controversy among the disciples. The issue then, and now, are so similar that the decision is as applicable to the latter as it was to the former. The former issue consisted in this, namely, an effort to have circumcision and the law of Moses inserted into the new covenant. The title to circumcision rested upon lineal descent.

The latter issue consists in this, namely, an effort to foist infant baptism into the new covenant or church. The title to infant baptism rests upon birthright—a believing paternity. So similar are circumcision and infant baptism, that the advocates for it claim that the latter came in room of the former. And, like their predecessors, they claim perpetuity, and universal obligation for the law of Moses.

The issue of A. D. 52, was, by mutual consent, referred to the apostles and elders at Jerusalem for decision. These, with the Holy Spirit presiding over their deliberations, vetoed both circumcision and the law of Moses. The record of this veto stands as directly against infant baptism as it did against circumcision. And as the apostolic veto stands against the law of Moses, therefore the defense of both is swept away.

It is a cause of devout gratitude that this controversy came while the apostles were yet alive. For, since their departure, the power to say yes or no, on questions or issues purely religious, is no longer in the church. And the apostles having placed their veto upon flesh, as being entitled to any consideration in the new order of things, therefore the question is settled.

But the first Judaizers appealed to the apostles, and then refused to abide their decision. It is therefore no marvel that their successors should be guilty of the same insubordination. Some questions never can be settled in all minds by authority. Notwithstanding, we do bless God for that apostolic council, and its decisions, and that we have an inspired record of it in the Book of Acts, fifteenth chapter. But for that a grievous Jewish yoke would have

been put upon the neck of the disciples. And perhaps the
report : "For it seemed good to the Holy Spirit, and to us,
to lay upon you no greater burden than these necessary
things," etc., may have saved the church from universal
Judaizing.

GENERAL REFLECTIONS.

THE Old Testament covenants of which we have been
speaking all looked to one grand consummation : a "new
and better covenant," "established upon better promises."
All the promises of all the old covenants, save this one, "in
thee shall all families of the earth be blessed," terminated
upon one family, were the property of one nation. The religion that grew out of these covenants was, therefore,
local and sectional. God, for wise and philanthropic purposes, designed that it should be a "wall of partition" between Jews and Gentiles. But "God, who worketh all
things after the counsel of his own will," determined in
himself, at the appointed time, to "break down this middle
wall." This is the major thought in the Epistle to the
Ephesians, to the seventeenth verse of the fourth chapter.
From this connected argument we read again with a little
abbreviation : "Wherefore remember, that ye being in time
past Gentiles in the flesh. That at that time ye (Gentiles)
were without Christ. Strangers from the covenants of
promise, having no hope, and without God in the world.
But now in Christ Jesus ye (Gentiles), who some time were
far off, are made nigh by the blood of Christ. For he is our
peace, who hath made both (Jew and Gentile) one, and
hath broken down the middle wall of partition between us
(Jews and Gentiles). Having abolished in his flesh the
enmity, even the law of commandments contained in ordinances, for to make in himself of the twain one new man,
so making peace. And that he might reconcile both (Jew
and Gentile) unto God in one body, by the cross, having
slain the enmity (of the law) thereby."

"Breaking down the middle wall of partition" stands in the text as antecedent, and "reconciling" those heretofore divided as consequent. All this was effected in "Christ," and "by Christ." "In thee shall all families of the earth be blessed."

This leads to the following conclusion, namely, That God purposed in Christ a universal religion. A religion in which all nations should stand upon perfect equality. This was intimated in the promise of Christ to Abraham : "All families of the earth be blessed," united, reconciled by one covenant, members of one body, Christ the "head."

But before this could be consummated, every thing local and sectional had to be taken out of the way. The last commission our Lord gave to the eleven was the beginning of this glorious consummation. "And he said unto them, Go preach the gospel to every creature. He that believeth and is baptized shall be saved, but he that believeth not shall be damned." "Every creature" is unlimited. Neither do the conditions, "believeth and is baptized," affect the universality. For, on the one hand, those who can not believe do not need salvation in the sense of pardon ; and on the other hand, they are not the subjects of this condemnation.

"Go preach the gospel." If the apostles had preached the "law," they would have preached it without a commission. Therefore, as we said before, they never preached the "law" to Jew or Gentile.

The commission, as recorded by Matthew, is prefaced by these remarkable words : "All power (authority) in heaven and in earth is given unto me." If all power belongs to Christ, then he can have no equal, no rival. Then, if the apostles had preached less or more than what is contained in the commission, they would have been rivals. For an omission or an addition would have been assumed responsibility. Preachers beware ! Jesus Christ will not suffer a rival. He claims the supremacy for himself.

"Teach, or convert all nations," is bold and aggressive.

3

"Baptizing them into the name of the Father, Son, and Spirit is uniting, bringing the converts of all nations under the same religious influence and supremacy. All antecedent covenants, laws, types, shadows, and prophecies were consummated in this last great converting, saving, uniting commission, by which the gospel was sent to the nations. The use the apostles made of the "things that were written aforetime," and the practical results of the gospel justify this conclusion.

Elias from heaven, and Moses from the regions of the dead, were never more highly honored than when they laid their commissions and honors at the feet of Jesus, when God said in their presence and hearing : "This is my Son, hear ye him." (Matt. xvii., 5.)

Could the Old Testament dispensation have been more highly honored than to meet the necessities of those under it, and then centre in Christ and the great salvation, and pass away? In this way Jesus Christ did not destroy the "law and the prophets," but honored, fulfilled, and magnified both.

To make them contribute to such an end was worthy of God who ordained them as instrumentalities to the introduction of a "better covenant," a "better hope," by which both Jews and Gentiles draw nigh to God. If all power in heaven and in earth were given unto the risen, victorious, triumphant Redeemer, he could not divide that power given to him with another. If he had acknowledged Moses and the prophets as sharers with him in the supremacy of "heaven and earth," they would have been his peers, his equals. When Jesus said : "All things must be fulfilled which were written in the law of Moses, and in the prophets, and in the psalms, concerning me," it shows the relation he assigned them, witnesses for him, not joint rulers or lawgivers. This was to honor them personally, and to stamp their writings with eternal truth and importance. Two laws and two lawgivers would be as unfeasible in one religion, as it is irrational. This would lead to endless and unadjustable claims and conflicts. Two presidents and two constitutions would be just as promotive of good, and of union in our civil government.

The first controversy in the church, as we have seen, originated in a division of authority between Jesus *the* Christ and Moses. And every division since A. D. 52 has been effected in the same way. Some pope, priest, bishop, or convention assumed the dictatorship. No sooner were these rivals of Jesus Christ sustained by the people, than the result was a division in the church. "There is one lawgiver." (James iv., 12.) The New Testament writings are pervaded with this unity. "One is your master," said Jesus to his disciples. The apostles made this the central fact in all their preaching. Peter, the apostle elect, to open the kingdom to the Jews and Gentiles said, and for the first time ever said : "God hath made that same Jesus whom you have crucified, both Lord and Christ, he is Lord of all," "the judge of quick and dead." (Acts x., 36–42.) Paul the apostle to the Gentiles, in the language of affectionate, earnest entreaty, says : "Keep the unity of the Spirit in the bond of peace. There is one body and one spirit, one hope of your calling, one Lord, one faith, one baptism, one God and Father of all, who is above all, and through all, and in you all." (Eph. iv.) This bond consists of seven items, each is a unit. This "bond of peace" is inspired. It was vouchsafed to the church by the "one Lord." Every other bond of peace in the church is an act of usurpation, and the authors wittingly or unwittingly are invading the prerogatives of Jesus Christ. The history of man-made bonds of union is but the history of schism, while the underlying secret is this, namely, that some leader desiring to draw disciples after him, disputed the exclusive authority with Christ, dictated new terms of church fellowship, and sometimes new conditions of salvation ; as for example, "Except ye be circumcised ye can not be saved." "Except ye present your infants in baptism you can not belong to our church." And if baptism is the door into the church, and if there is no salvation out of the church, then infant baptism is a condition of salvation. That there is no salvation out of the church, with some Scripture qualifications, is a universally admitted truth. But that infant baptism is a condition of admittance, or salvation, has ever been a contested proposition. In fact, there is no more need for it than there was or is for circumcision to the Gentiles.

The Scripture predicate at the head of this discourse-led us directly to an examination of the "covenants of promise." These covenants, though brief and simple in formal statement, are, nevertheless, comprehensive in meaning and of great doctrinal value.

The long and learned effort to identify the Old and New Testament covenants, churches, and the basis of membership has given great latitude, and involved the subject in almost hopeless entanglements. After a prayerful and laborious investigation of forty years, I am led to the irresistible conviction, that until the gospel is freed from these Jewish entanglements we shall have but indistinct views of the "hope of our calling" or Christian unity.

To do something in the way of clearing the subject, I had to let my range be, to some extent, commensurate with the controversial latitude of the subject.

Finally, brethren, remember that ye were Gentiles. "That at that time," before God sent the gospel to your fathers, "ye were without Christ," without "promise," without "hope," and "without God in the world." "But now you who were afar off are made nigh by the blood of Christ," the "blood of the new covenant." You are now in covenant with God. You have been "taken out" to be a "people for his name." You are in the reconstructed "tabernacle of David." You have God for the fulfillment of "exceeding great and precious promises," and God has you in your pledged obedience to him. God is your covenantor, and you are his covenantees. Remember, brethren, that God did once cast off a whole nation for the sin of covenant breaking. "They continued not in my covenant, and I regarded them not, saith the Lord." When you entered into covenant with God, when the "name of the Lord was called upon you," you said, "all that the Lord hath commanded that will we hear and that will we do." "Be faithful, and God will give you a crown of life." All the promises in Christ are covenanted mercies, hoped for on covenanted stipulations. This is the tenure by which you hold your title to mansions in the skies. This being so, you may know your standing before God and the ground of your hope.

And now a word to those who have not accepted the "new covenant" in the "blood of Christ." God, in sending the gospel to you, has laid this gracious covenant before you. Jesus Christ the Mediator asks you to accept it, to subscribe it with your own hand. And until you do, until the "name of the Lord is called upon you," you are Gentiles, aliens, "without hope and without God in the world." Does this describe your condition? If it does not, then there is no truth in the gospel. But if you believe the gospel, then you believe this to be your condition, namely, that you are "without hope and without God." Are you willing to die without hope and without God? Or have you given the subject no thought? You surely must die. One of two things will be true. In your dying hour you will have hope and God, or you will not. Make your choice now. If you have hope and God now, you will then. Just as you shall now decide, so it will be then. God has made the overture, but has left the final decision with you. I beseech you, then, be true to your convictions.

In the preceding pages the gospel is presented under the aspect of a covenant ; and obedience to the gospel under the aspect of covenanting—covenanting with God.

If you have read with attention you could not fail to see

this historic fact, that the belief of the gospel, "repentance" for sin, and "baptism in the name of the Lord Jesus" was the formal acceptance of the "new covenant." In this covenant both Jews and Gentiles had and still have promise of this great introductory blessing. "For I will be merciful to their unrighteousness, and their sins and iniquities will I remember no more." Have you the promise of "mercy and forgiveness?" If not, a period will turn up in your future history when you will wish you had.

APPEAL TO THE PEDOBAPTIST CLERGY.

THE subject suggests, and both duty and affection prompt, a few words to the Pedobaptist ministry. I have been where and as you are on the subject of infant baptism. Therefore what is in my heart I hope to speak advisedly. You have mainly depended upon the covenants, and especially the covenant of circumcision, for scriptural defense and support. But your witnesses are against you, "yourselves being judges." These you have long suborned to suit the necessities of the case. By this you have made them speak to the people what they do not say in their own "handwriting."

In word you have discarded the popish doctrine of "baptismal regeneration," but in your doctrinal standards and in your practice you hold to a kind of semi-infant baptismal regeneration by means of sprinkling a few drops of water on the face of an infant in the name of the Father, Son, and Holy Spirit. You have assigned eligibility for gospel blessings to the flesh, which belongs *only* to faith. In this you have placed the infant of a day upon an equality with the instructed believer in Christ, and elevated that which is born of the flesh, to that which is born of the Spirit. "That which is born of the flesh is flesh, and that which is born of the Spirit is spirit." (John iii., 6.)

Every gospel motive to an enlightened penitent believer

you have urged upon parents to offer their infant offspring to the Lord in baptism. For you do not baptize the believer for one object, and the infant for another. Whatever of grace or salvation baptism signifies to a believer you make it signify to an infant, for Jesus Christ gave but one commission to teach and baptize. Whatever of personal consecration, promise, hope, or spiritual enjoyment baptism secures to the believer you have therefore transferred to the baptized infant. You could do no less. For, in the absence of gospel motive, you could not make parents believe they were discharging a gospel duty.

What Papists and Episcopalians call regeneration, some of you call by another name. You may choose to call it a "sign and seal of ingrafting into Christ, of remission of sins," etc. But do you tell parents when you enforce this duty upon them that to their infants it is a sign of nothing, and a seal affixed to a blank? The difference between Catholics and Pedobaptist Protestants consists rather in a choice of words than a difference in meaning.

Bear with me. Your worthy views of the Christian religion, that spirituality you ascribe to every other act of Christian obedience and worship, turns up a palpable incongruity. For even the baptism of an adult unbeliever would be "form" only, without "power," there being no moral or spiritual fitness on the part of the candidate.

In this case, as in the case of infants, Paul would not define baptism to be the "washing of regeneration," there being no accompanying spiritual influence. In your creeds and sermons you make baptism the door of entrance into the church, and in the church you truly say there is salvation.

By the same initiative the infant and believer are brought into covenant, hence the oft-repeated phrase, "infant membership." This membership has created the necessity of the following classification of your church members : "communicants and *non*-communicants." This classification is a deception. It implies that the right of participancy in the Lord's supper is the only difference between them. But this is far from being true. You withhold from the latter class the *grace* of church *censure* and *discipline*. And that is not all, you do not grant them the right of suffrage or petition. And as respects Christian rights, honors, or privileges, you treat them as aliens. This is prudential. Inasmuch as some of your church organisms are democratic, and the non-communicants are usually a majority, they could therefore have things in their own way. The classification in your case is wise, but, nevertheless, it is a deception, and as respects the church of the New Testament it is as irrational as it is unscriptural. Your holding with obstinacy to the Jewish doctrine of "sanctified flesh," abolished in Christ, the substitution of this *flesh* for faith, by which the regenerating power of the gospel is brought to bear upon the sinner's heart and conscience, has led you into all these palpable blunders. And when we consider the relation between baptism and the "new covenant in the blood of Christ," a relation you acknowledge when you say "baptism is a seal of the covenant of grace," your mistake may be fatal.

But before I close this appeal, let me call your attention briefly to some of the consequences that have grown out of this early departure from the "simplicity there is in Christ."

Baptism, the first act of overt obedience to Jesus Christ has become so involved in the claims and conflicts of rival parties, that it can only be rescued from its present entanglements by throwing aside the work of long centuries and beginning anew. Read and ponder well the following :

From the *British Standard* of September 9, 1864, "Charles II. Spurgeon and the Clergy," No. 2, the editor, who is himself a Pedobaptist, says : "Nothing can be more unsatisfactory than the views which prevail among the various bodies of non-conformists or dissenters on the ordinance of baptism. A picture might be drawn of the diversity which exists of a most startling character. ' That diversity, in fact, is such, seeing that truth is *one*, as almost to excite a doubt whether all denominations be not more or less in error with respect to it. The chief views may be thus expressed, from which it will be seen how contradictory each is to the other. Baptism took the place of circumcision ; the baptism of children is founded on the Abrahamic covenant ; only the children of believers ought to be baptized ; baptism only requires that the parents should make a general profession of Christianity to entitle their infants to baptism ; baptism introduces the child to the church, and entitles it to superintendence and instruction ; baptism leaves the recipient in a state of isolation from any local church, and only brings them into unison with the church generally."

To this extract, I will add a few from Henry Ward Beecher's sermon on baptism : " I concede, and I assert, first, that infant baptism is nowhere commanded in the New Testament. No man can find a passage that commands it ; and if it can stand only on that ground, we may as well give it up first as last." " It is not safe to found it on the practice of the apostles, in the baptism of Christian families." " I assert that the doctrine that, as a Christian ordinance, it is a substitute for the circumcision of the Jews, is a doctrine that is utterly untenable, to say nothing more." " If any body asks me, where is your text for baptizing children ? I reply, there is none. And if I am asked, then why do you baptize them ? I say, because it is found to be beneficial. And if men say to me, do you think the baptism of children is a divine ordinance ? My reply is, that I believe an ox-yoke is a divine ordinance."

The foregoing extracts only set forth some of the " contradictory" views between some of the Pedobaptist ministry. Then there are the thousand and one conflicting opinions between the high and low churchmen on the question of baptismal regeneration. The first, understanding

and administering the baptismal service in a most literal
sense ; and the latter taking the text at a large discount,
perhaps by construction, meaning only "sign of regeneration." However you may differ on the general subject, you
are compelled to agree either in unqualified infant baptismal regeneration, or retain the thing in embryo. For even
Mr. Beecher concedes all that Papist or Protestant could
ask. He says, " And though the child does not understand
what is being done in the act of baptism, that does not alter
the fact that God's Spirit dwells in and moves upon the
heart of that child."

Mark the language, " *that child*." The " Spirit of God"
did not then " dwell in" and " move upon the heart of that
child" before the act of baptism ; if so, " *that child*" is a
sophism, and if the Spirit of God does not " dwell in" and
" move upon" the hearts of unbaptized infants, and does
"dwell in" and "move upon" the hearts of baptized infants,
then Mr. Beecher, High Churchmen, and Roman Catholics
are right on this question, and infant " baptismal regeneration" is a Bible truth !

The preceding extracts from two eminent Pedobaptist
ministers are suggestive. The first says there is a great
"diversity of views," "contradictory, each to the other."
He says this fact is " startling, seeing that truth is *one*,"
and hence concludes that "all denominations are in error".
on the subject of baptism. He has very clearly set forth
that they agree among themselves in one thing *only*,
namely, that infants should be baptized while they differ
in every thing else pertaining to the subject.

The latter extracts from the somewhat *eccentric* but
candid Beecher give the reason of this "diversity" and
" contradiction" among the advocates of infant baptism.
He is the first that has denied to it any scriptural counte-
nance and support, but still persisted in the practice. He
says : " There is no command for it ;" " the families baptized by the apostles furnish no evidence ;" " that baptism

came in the room of Jewish circumcision is utterly untenable." " If I am asked for a text, I say there is none," etc., and therefore says, and *logically* says : " If the practice must be founded upon Scripture authority, we may as well give it up first as last."

But Mr. Beecher informs us that he continues the administration upon an assumed hypothetical benefit to infants. He shows that there is a beautiful parallel between the utility of infant baptism and an ox-yoke, they both being " divine ordinances."

With Mr. Beecher, then, infant baptism is purely an ecclesiastical affair, resting upon human authority. In things of this kind one man's opinion is as good as another, and one man's authority is equal to that of another. In Mr. Beecher's honest surrender of all Bible authority the editor of the *British Standard* will find the real cause of that endless " diversity" and " contradiction" existing among Pedobaptists. They can not disguise the fact that the complications of the subject are assuming a serious form. They have too much faith to abandon the ordinance altogether, and not enough to preach and practice it as the apostles did.

As I hinted before, you must begin anew. You must throw away your entire Pedobaptist literature, and return to the apostolic order. There is no other help for you. You know your advocacy of this subject has ever been an apple of discord among yourselves, to say nothing of the graver issues between you and the advocates of believers' baptism. This feature of your system is virtually Judaizing, and inherently schismatical. We say this upon your own testimony. In the exercise of this freedom, we gratify no partisan feeling. Nay, we esteem you. We hold many of you, both the living and the dead, in veneration for your learning and piety.

In religion, not as in science, men usually are advocates before they are investigators. This has been my own experie   Children usually, as they should, accept the religious instructions of their parents without distrust, and therefore often become the advocates of systems received by tradition from their fathers. On this ground I can account for the long continuance of this human device—this convenient proselyting dogma, by means of which you take time by the "forelock." On this ground only can we reconcile your large intelligence and devotion to Christianity, with your persistent effort to perpetuate this early departure from the apostolic faith and practice.

Will it always be so? It will not. Let me call your attention to that class of persons who were called Anabaptists in the days of Luther, and afterward, and to Roger Williams and his little band. Few in number—poor and despised by all. Both Papists and Protestants united in fixing upon them the most odious heresies to justify, as they claimed, persecution unto death.

I need not tell you that these "heresies," once so very obnoxious, have now become respectable, and have found their way into the temples of orthodoxy ; for, by the consent of all, an immersed believer is a free-born citizen of the kingdom of heaven. With all this tremendous odds against them, the advocates of believers' baptism have grown in numbers, and every thing that gives weight and influence to Christian character. They have received large accessions per annum from your communicants and non-communicants, while you have received, perhaps, not one in a century from them by proselytism. These facts, "known and read of all men," indicate a providential direction, and the tendency of the popular religious mind. I pray you do not charge this freedom to partisan feeling. If the few words the author has addressed to you are but empty puerilities, treat them as such. If these pages shall tend, even in a limited degree, to enlighten the reader on this great introductory subject, to the Lord we shall give all the praise.

www.ingramcontent.com/pod-product-compliance
Lightning Source LLC
Chambersburg PA
CBHW031746090426
42739CB00008B/899